The Life, Times & Music® Series

The Life, Times & Music® Series

Judith Mahoney Pasternak

DEDICATION

When I was fourteen, my father, Bill Mahoney, decided it was time for me to learn jazz. So he sat me down in front of the record player—it wasn't a stereo yet—and put on Jelly Roll Morton singing "Mamie's Blues" and Mezz Mezzrow, Sidney Bechet, and Tommy Ladnier playing "Really the Blues."

He had timed it exactly right. I was old enough and young enough for the music to crack my heart in two. Thanks, Bill—this is for you.

ACKNOWLEDGMENTS

And thanks, too, to Richard Barr for giving this book the benefit of his jazz expertise, and to Nathaniel Marunas for his extraordinary ability to know exactly how a writer would have said something if she had had her wits about her when she wrote it.

A FRIEDMAN/FAIRFAX BOOK
© 1995 Friedman/Fairfax Publishers
All rights reserved. No part of this publication may be reproduced, stored in a retrieval system, or transmitted, in any form or by any means, electronic, mechanical, photocopying, recording, or otherwise, without prior written permission from the publisher.

ISBN 1-56799-235-8

Editor: Nathaniel Marunas
Art Director: Jeff Batzli
Designer: Tanya Ross-Hughes
Cover Design: Zemsky Design
Photography Editor: Colleen A. Branigan
Production Manager: Jeanne E. Kaufman

Grateful acknowledgment is given to authors, publishers, and photographers for permission to reprint material. Every effort has been made to determine copyright owners of photographs and illustrations. In the case of any omissions, the publishers will be pleased to make suitable acknowledgments in future editions.

Printed in the United States of America by Quebecor Printing Semline, Inc.

For bulk purchases and special sales, please contact:
Friedman/Fairfax Publishers
Attention: Sales Department
15 West 26th Street
New York, NY 10010
(212) 685-6610 FAX (212) 685-1307

website: *http://www.webcom.com/~friedman/*

Contents

Introduction: An American Child 6

Legacy of the Diaspora 10

Blacks in Blackface: The Minstrel Shows 14

Ragtime: Professors and Piano Rolls 18

Singin' the Blues 22

Only in New Orleans 27

Is It Jazz Yet? New Orleans, 1900–1917 32

Far from Dixie: The Original Dixieland Jazz Bands, 1915–1926 40

New Orleans North: South Side Chicago, 1917–1924 43

Jazz, Chicago Style: 1922–1928 46

Still Going: The Dixieland Revival, 1942–1995 53

Coda: Beyond Dixie—Big Bands, Boogie-Woogie, Bebop 58

Bibliography 60

Suggested Reading 61

Suggested Listening 62

Index 63

introduction:
An American Child

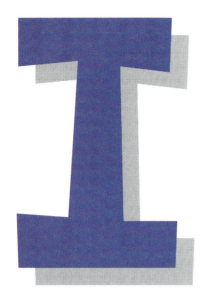

In an irate letter to the jazz magazine Downbeat *in the late 1930s, aging jazz giant Jelly Roll Morton attempted to correct the then-current perception of "St. Louis Blues" composer W.C. Handy (1873–1958) as the originator of jazz.*

Wrote Morton, "I myself happened to be the creator of jazz, in the year of 1902."

The date was more or less correct, but Morton's self-described role in the creation of jazz was a characteristic exaggeration. Certainly Morton had been a creator of jazz, but he wasn't even among its first generation. He claimed to have been born in 1890, which would have made him twelve years old in 1902; at that time there were others already shaping the new music that was rising from the American South. Morton would have his turn as an innovator, but neither he nor any other single person "created" jazz.

Jazz wasn't created. It evolved, a native child of black and white America, its distant ancestry comprising elements as diverse as West African tribal funeral rites and Napoleon's marching bands. Along with so many other facets of U.S. life, black and white, jazz rose out of slavery and the African diaspora; it came from the nation's rivers and deltas, its cities and plantations; and it was spread by the peregrinations of Americans up and down and across the country. Its immediate parents were minstrelsy, ragtime, and the blues.

Jazz wasn't the first native American music; indigenous peoples of the North American continent sang, danced, and drummed long before the coming of Europeans or Africans. But jazz was the first cultural product of the great American melting pot. Jass, or jazz, was formed from the extraordinarily complex interactions between European and African traditions that came to a boil in New Orleans just after the turn of the century.

An American Child

Virtually as soon as jazz had a name, it had different schools, distinguished by and large by being played by either black or white—but not mixed—bands. The term Dixieland jazz *was coined by the all-white bands that were the first to make and sell gramophone records. When black musicians began recording—by then, many of them had moved north—their music was given the name of its homeland and called "New Orleans jazz." The New Orleans–born Morton had been on the spot when jazz began; that much was true. So had hundreds of other musicians. Most fell nameless into that turbulent, emphatically nonlinear history; a few left us their names and their tunes.*

This is their story.

On the streets of New Orleans in the first decade of the twentieth century, many disparate elements came together into a new and wholly American music: jazz.

Jelly's Blues: Jelly Roll Morton (1890?–1941)

Jelly Roll Morton probably composed the first written jazz music, which may explain why he came to think of himself as its creator.

Morton's origins, like those of jazz itself, are shrouded in myth, mystery, and some deliberate mystification. He was born Ferdinand Lemott (or Lementhe) in New Orleans in either 1885 or 1890. (The later date is more commonly accepted but somewhat incongruous with accounts of his playing piano in Storyville, New Orleans' famed official red-light district, by 1902.)

Morton was a Creole of color, one of the French-speaking, light-skinned descendants of free blacks and children of French settlers who saw themselves as the aristocrats of black New Orleans. But he was more comfortable with the French side of his ancestry than with the African side, which he sometimes tried to deny altogether.

In the bubbling cauldron of musical invention that was the New Orleans of his childhood and youth, every brothel of quality in Storyville had its piano player, a career Jelly Roll pursued until roughly his twentieth birthday. By 1906, he reputedly made a munificent fifteen to eighteen dollars a night, though he also earned money by playing in minstrel shows (he was not a successful

Jelly Roll Morton in Chicago, 1923, at the dawn of black jazz recording.

An American Child

comedian); by publishing music; and, outside the music and theater world, by hustling pool, promoting boxing, and occasionally pimping. The young man started calling himself "Morton" to disassociate his family from his seedier pursuits.

About the same time, Morton began writing music. Along with other musicians, he was fusing elements of ragtime, blues and marches into what would soon enough be called "jazz," though at that point it was new and had no name of its own. His first known composition was "New Orleans Blues." Not long after he wrote it, he left New Orleans on the first leg of what would be a lifelong ramble around the country. He wrote "Alabama Bound" in Mobile; his first published composition (and possibly the first published jazz composition ever), "Jelly Roll Blues," was printed in Chicago in 1915.

By 1923, with Morton in Chicago again, the word *jazz* was known across the nation and would shortly come to characterize the decade itself. It was around this time that Jelly Roll made his first recordings, for the Gennett Company: piano solos like "King Porter Stomp" (later a Benny Goodman big band hit), "New Orleans Joys," and "Wolverine Stomp," along with at least one title, "Milenberg Joys," recorded with the (all-white) New Orleans Rhythm Kings.

By 1926, Jelly Roll had put together the band he called the Red Hot Peppers, with which he signed a two-year Victor recording contract. The Peppers played composed, tightly arranged (by Morton)—rather than improvisational—jazz. Recordings like "The Pearls," "Dead Man Blues," and "Sidewalk Blues" made them Victor's top-selling "hot" band.

In 1928, Morton went to New York. But the era of New Orleans jazz had peaked, and Victor didn't renew his contract. The growing popularity of big bands made it harder for him to find work, and things got worse when the Depression hit. For ten years, he played where he could—in vaudeville orchestras and in small clubs in New York and Washington, D.C.

By 1938, he was either pushing fifty or just past it (depending on whether he had been born in 1885 or 1890). They had been hard years: like many jazz players, Jelly Roll was wearing out young. He had respiratory and heart problems, and he thought his contributions to jazz were being forgotten.

That year, however, he was "discovered"—or rediscovered—in a D.C. club by Alan Lomax, then the folklore curator at the Library of Congress. Entranced by Jelly Roll's music and his astonishing flow of reminiscences (some of it fictional) of jazz history, Lomax made a project of getting it all down on wax and on paper.

Lomax oversaw a series of recordings for the Library of Congress. Morton, recording for what turned out to be the last time, played piano, as he had done at the beginning. He talked, as he had always done. And—for the first and only time, at least on record—he sang. On a half-dozen sides of almost unbearable poignancy, he played and sang haunting two- and three-minute blues about New Orleans in the early days. These included "Mamie's Blues," which he said he had learned in the brothels from New Orleans blues singer Mamie Desdoumes, and "Buddy Bolden's Blues," about some of the first jazz men. Out of the conversations, Lomax later wove together a Morton autobiography called *Mr. Jelly Roll*.

The Library of Congress recordings and *Mr. Jelly Roll* may have assuaged Morton's still-fierce pride, but they didn't restart his faded career. In 1940, he made his last trip, to Los Angeles. He died there the next year.

Legacy of the Diaspora

The polyrhythms of African drumming, the call-and-response of African chants, the five-tone scale of African music, the gods and goddesses of African religions—all these elements are part of the American potpourri that became jazz. Yet they wound up there because of an American paradox that lies at the heart of jazz history: had there been no slavery, there would have been no jazz.

Jazz was born of the meeting of African and European culture and music, having passed through two transformative filters. The first was two centuries of slavery in America, made possible by the widespread traffic in slaves between Africa—especially West Africa—and the Western Hemisphere, and the consequent involuntary dispersion of Africans throughout the hemisphere. The second filter was some three decades of reconstruction and freedom that followed the official end of slavery.

When the grim ships landed here with their human cargo—or, more precisely, with that fraction of their cargo that survived the horrific journey across the Middle Passage—they brought not only many peoples of Africa, but also their cultures. Enslaved, torn from their homelands and families, the Africans tenaciously retained whatever facets of their various cultures they could.

Their ability to retain their cultural identity depended in part on who their masters were. The enslavers were no more homogenous than the enslaved. Different European peoples—the British, the French, the Spanish—tended to import their slaves from distinct parts of Africa. The English took their slaves largely from the Ashanti peoples of what is now Ghana, the Spanish from the Yorubans, the French from the Dahomeans of what is now Benin.

Different Europeans also treated their slaves differently. For example, the Protestants of northern European background tended to Christianize their slaves more assiduously than did the Spanish and the French. African religious traditions therefore had a higher survival rate in the predominantly Catholic sections of the New World—South America, the Caribbean, and the southern Mississippi regions of the United States—than in the Protestant sections.

So while most of the Ashanti traditions disappeared or went underground, Yoruba religion and lore survived in Cuba and other Spanish possessions, as did the religions of Dahomey—including Voudun (or voodoo) in Haiti and Martinique—and, most significantly for the future of American

Like so many facets of U.S. culture, black and white, jazz has roots in the fields and plantations of the Old South.

music, in Louisiana. (Also, the animistic African religions blended more easily with Catholicism, with its shrines and votive statues, than into the starker Protestant sects, so many Cuban, Haitian, and Louisianian slaves became, so to speak, Yoruba-Catholics or Voudun-Catholics.)

The other major factor in the survival or repression of elements of African culture was whether the slave owners perceived a particular cultural expression as dangerous to them. (They saw none as valuable.) The traditions the owners saw as hazardous they tried ruthlessly to suppress. Throughout the hemisphere the potential use of the drum for communication was seen as threatening, for instance, and many slave-owning communities banned African drumming.

Call-and-response chants, however, were as functional in the work of slaves as they had been in the course of heavy work in Africa, and the slave masters and overseers had no quarrel with their slaves' use of chants—field hollers—to make work rhythmic and more efficient. The improvisational nature of African music also survived in those chants, which became one strand in the ancestry of gospel, blues, and jazz. In the English-owned plantations north and east of Louisiana, the improvised call-and-response chants made their way into the slaves' Protestant liturgies as well, blending with the "lining-out" style of white hymn-singing in which a minister called out the words and a congregation sang them back and embellished them.

Dixieland

Finally, into the songs of the slaves there crept new notes altogether, the so-called blues tonality that flats the third and seventh notes of the seven-note (diatonic) European scale. Some musicologists have hypothesized that blues tonality grew out of the superimposition of the diatonic scale over the five-note African scale. However it came about, jazz would not have been jazz without it.

The importation of African slaves into the Americas began early in the seventeenth century. It was outlawed in the United States in 1808, but the ban no more ended the slave trade than did Prohibition stop the sale of alcohol and drinking a little over a century later. A clandestine traffic in African slaves went on virtually until Emancipation in 1863. And throughout the nineteenth century, planters and other slave owners immigrated to the Americas from the Caribbean, bringing their slaves with them, so that American-born Africans—not yet African Americans—were continually brought into touch with African-born slaves.

Thus slavery brought into the still-young United States many of the first threads of the nation's own music. In the cities and on the rivers, freed slaves, their descendants, and the descendants of Europeans would weave those threads into the fabric of jazz.

Cotton Pickers, by W.H. Johnson (1901–1971). In the 1940s Johnson, like his contemporary Jacob Lawrence, turned to painting scenes from African American history.

The End of a Perfect Death: The New Orleans Jazz Funeral

A somber parade of African American pallbearers and mourners march a coffin through the streets, the pace set by a band heavy on the brass playing a solemn, dirge-tempo "Just a Closer Walk with Thee."

An hour later, the parade returns, minus the coffin. But the atmosphere has changed. The music is upbeat, exuberant, even rambunctious: "Didn't He Ramble?" or "When the Saints Go Marching In." The erstwhile mourners dance.

It's a New Orleans jazz funeral, a contemporary expression of ancient African religious traditions filtered through European Protestantism, the blend expressed by a jazz/marching band, itself another New Orleans institution.

The marching band came from Napoleon's France to New Orleans just after the French sold the city to Thomas Jefferson in 1803. The heart of the city still belonged to France, and the march mania spread from New Orleans' French-descended upper classes through its Creoles of color to, ultimately, its darkest, most African population, which adapted the marches to its own purposes.

Many non-French-speaking African Orleanians still believed, as had their African ancestors, that this life is only part of the spectrum of life itself, and death is thus a passage from one phase to another—a passage that rite and ritual can ease for the newly deceased. Their funerals, like the funerals of the tribes from which they came, encompassed not only mourning the dead and celebrating the life that had ended, but also putting on a good show to speed the deceased on his or her way.

The good show involved the march to the graveside and the return therefrom,

"Oh, when the saints come marching in...."
Draped in flowers, the Grand Marshal leads a jazz funeral through the streets of New Orleans.

followed by a feast. African Orleanians formed hundreds of secret societies, mutual insurance fraternities that assured the availability of funds for the march and the feast. As jazz developed at the beginning of this century, the best funerals came more and more to include the new music.

Jazz was well suited for funerals. Its arrangements were rooted in the 4/4 rhythm of the marching band and its orchestration was, like the marching band, heavy on the brass; its tunes were often new arrangements of familiar old songs. The musicians were paid to play the cortege to and from the graveside, but the whole neighborhood, including musicians who weren't working that funeral, got to share in the feast.

As Jelly Roll Morton once noted, a really good funeral was "the end of a perfect death."

blacks in blackface: The Minstrel Shows

Minstrel shows, the predecessors of vaudeville, were one of the breeding grounds for jazz. These moveable feasts were also where the ironies and contradictions of black and white America multiplied and twisted, singing and dancing all the way.

American minstrelsy was a performance tradition popular around the nation for the half century centered around the Civil War.

In the first twenty-five years of the minstrel shows, white men put burnt cork on their faces, played instruments rooted in Africa, and delivered their impressions of the music, dialect, and style of the enslaved race. After the Civil War, newly freed blacks joined new troupes and performed in all-black minstrel shows—in which they also put burnt cork on their faces, played the same instruments, and delivered white impresarios' and writers' impressions of blacks.

Though the minstrel show in its final form flourished from 1850 to 1870, documentation exists of blackface impersonations as far back as 1810. In Tennessee and elsewhere on the western frontier, whites donned burnt cork and danced to the music of bone clappers, tambourines, and banjos. (The clappers and tambourines—and, almost certainly, the dances—were African imports; the banjo was a black American variant on an African instrument.)

Around 1828, a white man in Louisville named Tom or Tim Rice founded a career

Among the better jobs African American men could get from the post–Civil War era to the first decades of the twentieth century were with the railroad, which became a major conduit for the spread of African American culture. Consequently, the Pullman porter and the station porter, or "redcap," were stock characters in many minstrel shows, like this one (circa 1915).

The Minstrel Shows

on his imitation of an obviously African dance he saw performed by an aged slave called—whatever his name had been in Africa—Uncle Jim. Uncle Jim's master's last name—and, therefore, Uncle Jim's last name—was Crow, and the old man called the song he sang as he danced "Jump, Jim Crow." The name would pass into history through Rice's early-minstrel version of the song and dances.

Gertrude "Ma" Rainey and a colleague strike a tableau in a Rabbit Foot Minstrels performance.

Sometime in the 1840s, minstrelsy crossed the Atlantic. The English writer William Makepeace Thackeray (1811–1863) was deeply moved by a performance he saw in London. His friend Charles Dickens (1812–1870) reported on a minstrel show he saw in the United States during his American tour. Dickens had witnessed what was at that point a rarity: a black minstrel in a white troupe, probably William Henry Lane (1825?–1862), whose stage name was Juba.

By the decade before the war, the minstrel show was the most popular form of commercial entertainment in the nation and the source of much of the country's popular music. (Stephen Foster was only one of hundreds of composers writing songs for minstrel performances.) Touring groups like Edwin P. Christy's (1815–1862) Minstrels crossed each others' paths in small towns and cities, north and south, east and west. The format had become standardized, consisting of an opening parade, a vaudeville or "olio" free-for-all, and a burlesque of a well-known play or opera. (Shakespeare was a favorite target, but the single most frequently parodied drama was *Uncle Tom's Cabin*.)

The war and Emancipation did not dim the popularity of the medium, but they did add one more layer of irony: the troupes of blacks in blackface. Black minstrels did not wipe off the burnt cork until around 1890.

Also about that time the last generation of minstrels joined the parade: the men and women who would create out of the by-then fading embers of minstrelsy three separate and distinct American performance media.

Dixieland

Among the white singers and dancers, minstrelsy faded almost imperceptibly into vaudeville. The musicians, black and white, became the progenitors of the music that would be called jazz. And the black singers—many of them women—turned to the blues.

The list of minstrel performers of the early twentieth century who became early jazz and blues stars is staggering. "Papa" Jack Laine (George Vitelle Laine, 1873–1966) led an early jazz band in a minstrels' orchestra pit in the late 1890s. Jelly Roll Morton performed (badly, they said) with McCabe's Minstrels about ten years later. And the "Father," "Mother," and "Empress" of the blues all worked in minstrel shows: W.C. Handy was a member of the Mahara's Minstrels in 1895, before he wrote (or wrote down) "St. Louis Blues"; Gertrude "Ma" Rainey was the star of Rainey's Rabbit Foot Minstrels; and her protégé, Bessie Smith (1895–1937), sang in Rainey's show beginning in about 1912. The United States was becoming more sophisticated, culturally and technologically. Vaudeville was replacing the minstrel shows as a live performance medium and records were popularizing music around the country. African Americans no longer had to put on blackface to appear before audiences.

Whites used blackface for a longer period. Well into the vaudeville era, stars like Al Jolson (1888–1950) and Eddie Cantor (1892–1964)—and hundreds of now-forgotten entertainers—performed in blackface. The burnt cork sat next to the greasepaint on the makeup shelf for almost another half century, long after minstrelsy had faded away.

Minstrel to Bluesman: W.C. Handy, 1873–1958

William Christopher Handy's long, prodigious career began with a minstrel troupe and ended with Hollywood's first biography of an African American, the understandably erroneous premise of which was that Handy was the "Father of the Blues."

Handy didn't father the blues. He only discovered them, as did many others between 1900 and World War I. Other people wrote them down, but Handy copyrighted them, and his tunes made him one of America's most popular songwriters for almost fifty years.

No one knows exactly how many of Handy's hundreds of songs he actually wrote and how many he merely adapted from folk sources. But his real accomplishment was *publishing* the blues—the only way, just before the advent of the recording era, to popularize them.

Born in Alabama in 1873 into a family of deep Methodist conviction, Handy was taught that secular music was the Devil's work. In the 1890s, however, music and minstrelsy were among the few expanding fields of endeavor for African Americans, and Handy joined Mahara's Minstrels when he was twenty-two. His father said he would rather have seen him dead.

By 1896 Handy was the troupe's cornet soloist and bandleader. A few years later he was conducting small dance bands, still without having shed the prejudices of his Methodist training. He only approved of refined, lightly classical- and march-oriented music. Ragtime he dismissed as "rhythm without melody." (Jazz as a musical genre was still in the future.)

When he heard the blues in 1903 Handy changed his mind. He found them "primitive" but "haunting," and began writing them down, then making up new ones.

In 1912 Handy published his first hit song, "Memphis Blues." Two years later he released what would become the single best-known blues title ever, "St. Louis Blues." Not a real blues and possibly not his own creation, it nevertheless made him famous and enabled him to start his own music publishing business in Memphis.

In 1918 he moved to New York, where he continued to publish, write, and play. Late in the 1920s, Columbia Records promoted him as their answer to the Original Dixieland Jazz Band. And in 1929, his most famous song was used as the basis for a seventeen-minute film, the only one in which the incomparable Bessie Smith ever appeared.

Handy's vision began to fail, though he was still recording as late as 1939, when he was sixty-six. In 1943, not long after the publication of an autobiography called *Father of the Blues*, he suffered a terrible mishap: he fell onto the New York City subway tracks. The injuries—from which he never entirely recovered—further impaired his mobility, and he was ill and near-reclusive for the rest of his life.

William Christopher Handy died early in 1958, the year Hollywood released the second *St. Louis Blues* movie, based on Handy's life and starring Nat "King" Cole and Cab Calloway.

The hundreds of songs W.C. Handy penned during his long career include—besides the world-famous "St. Louis Blues"—"Beale Street Blues" and "Atlanta Blues."

Dixieland

ragtime: Professors and Piano Rolls

Minstrelsy evolved across the United States over half a century, but ragtime burst onto the American music scene with explosive force at a particular moment.

It came primarily out of the Midwest at the end of the nineteenth century, with the publication of Tom Turpin's (1873–1922) "Harlem Rag" in 1897. Turpin had struck gold. Within weeks, half the songwriters in the country were dipping into the ragtime lode, including one man who would become the most famous of ragtime composers, Scott Joplin.

But Joplin didn't publish until two years after Turpin had launched ragtime. In 1899—the same year a sixteen-year-old in Baltimore, Eubie Blake (James Hubert Blake), began an eighty-year career with his first rag—Joplin published the "Maple Leaf Rag." It sold seventy-five thousand copies in the next twelve months, made Joplin's fortune, and carried ragtime across the ocean to Europe.

Unlike jazz, which was developing at the same time (and would get part of its form from ragtime and part of its impetus from the ragtime craze), ragtime didn't seem to need a vibrant, geographically distinct community of like-minded musicians for its sudden evolution. Tom Turpin was from St. Louis, as were ragtime composers Louis Chauvin and Artie Mathews; Scott Joplin was from nearby Sedalia; but young Eubie Blake was halfway across the country.

Ragtime was a solo pursuit that required musical training and literacy but not musical accompaniment. The music was composed in the European tradition but with a hint of Africa in its continued syncopation. It was not jazz—which was improvisational at its heart—but it was one of the two immediate predecessors of jazz (the other was the blues). And ragtime was the first American music written in virtually equal numbers by white and black composers.

Exactly what was ragtime? In its original, pure form, it was essentially syncopated march music for solo piano. (The American March King, John Philip Sousa [1854–1932], was making brass arrangements of ragtime compositions for his own band by 1900.) That is, a rag was a composition in march time (2/4) that maintained the march beat in the bass (the left hand) while the right hand played an 8-beat-to-the-bar melody with an accent on every *third* beat.

Professors and Piano Rolls

The composition of ragtime required musical literacy and sophistication; playing it credibly required the same, along with considerable skill as a piano player. (Joplin himself was reputed to be only a mediocre performer of his own work.) By the turn of the century, the best (and some of the worst) pianists were recording it on piano rolls, and the piano "professors" who entertained in brothels were performing ragtime in every dive around the country. Joplin's first rags were composed for fellow piano players at the Maple Leaf Club, a Sedalia professors' rendezvous; his bittersweet melodies were big hits in the brothels.

A ragtime dance, circa 1911, when ragtime was viewed as exuberant, convention-defying—even decadent—music.

Ragtime came to a peak and a turning point in New Orleans. The brass, minstrel, and marching bands took it up: John Robichaux (before 1875–after 1910) and "Papa" Jack Laine, both of whom had early jazz bands, were playing ragtime arrangements immediately after the turn of the century. Much of Jelly Roll Morton's early music also elaborated on ragtime syncopation; he recorded Joplin's own "Maple Leaf Rag" more than once. One musicologist has described Dixieland jazz itself as "orchestrated ragtime."

Within a decade other music genres were adapting and absorbing ragtime at home and abroad. "Alexander's Ragtime Band" became pop songwriter Irving Berlin's (1888–1989) first great hit in 1911. In Europe, composers Claude Debussy and Igor Stravinsky both wrote ragtime-influenced music, Debussy for the "Golliwog's Cakewalk" section of his

"Children's Corner" Suite (1906–1908) and Stravinsky, a little later, in "Ragtime" (1918) and "Piano Rag Music" (1919). In New York City, in the hands of pianists like James P. Johnson (1894–1955) and Willie "The Lion" Smith (1897–1973), ragtime evolved into the music called "house-party" or "Harlem" piano style.

But pure ragtime faded quickly from the music scene. Joplin's ambitious ragtime opera, *Treemonisha*, produced in 1915, was perhaps both a climax and a farewell to the genre.

Ragtime would see a massive revival almost seventy years later, inspired by the use of Joplin's "The Entertainer" in the soundtrack of the enormously popular film *The Sting* (1974). Music scholars like Joshua Rifkin made new recordings of dozens of Joplin's rags and those of other ragtime composers. Eubie Blake took up his pen again at ninety, and for a couple of years, audiences listened to ragtime again.

No one seemed to notice the anachronistic nature of *The Sting*'s ragtime soundtrack: the action of the film takes place during the Great Depression of the 1930s, when swing was king and ragtime was twenty years in the past.

Ragtime in Two Keys: Scott Joplin (1868–1917) and Eubie Blake (1883–1983)

Scott Joplin's brief, meteoric career began and ended with ragtime; Eubie Blake's began with ragtime and moved through half a dozen American musical genres over eighty years. Joplin died at forty-nine, heartbroken and embittered by his failure to lift ragtime beyond its popularity into the realm of serious music; Blake got just what he wanted: popular success.

Born fifteen years and half a continent apart, they nevertheless began writing ragtime at about the same time. By the time he was thirty, Joplin was an established, successful piano player and songwriter. After an extensive classical education from a European

Sixty years after Scott Joplin's death, such ragtime compositions as "Maple Leaf Rag" and "The Entertainer" were finally perceived as serious American music.

piano teacher in his east Texas birthplace, he had moved to St. Louis while still in his teens. In 1894 he settled in Sedalia and toured the country alone and with a quartet. In 1899, he named a rag after the Maple Leaf Club and handed it over to publisher John Stark. It made Stark—and Joplin—comfortable, if not rich.

Eubie Blake wrote his first rag in 1899, the same year "Maple Leaf Rag" was published. Only sixteen years old, he had learned the piano under very different circumstances from Joplin's: in the brothels of Baltimore, the city of his birth. But by 1899, Blake was moving up in the world and was soon playing popular dance music in medicine shows and hotels.

"Maple Leaf Rag" was the first in an unbroken string of ragtime hits for Joplin. Over the next decade he published almost thirty, including "Elite Syncopation" and "The Entertainer," but success was not enough. He wanted to raise ragtime from the dance hall to the concert hall. He wrote a full-length ballet score, The Ragtime Dance, and produced it in Sedalia's Woods Opera House. Three years later, he wrote his first (unsuccessful) ragtime opera, The Guest of Honor.

Joplin had other sources of anguish: his failing marriage collapsed after the death of his infant child. He left Sedalia and moved several times, ending up in New York in 1907. There the last disaster—in the form of syphilis—struck.

Increasingly ill and increasingly obsessive, he spent eight years trying to launch his most ambitious work, the ragtime opera Treemonisha. Finally, in 1915, he produced a single concert performance, which failed to overwhelm the public.

By 1916, incapacitated by disease, Scott Joplin was placed in New York's prisonlike Ward's Island Hospital, where he died of syphilis in 1917.

While Joplin lay dying, Blake was touring the United States in vaudeville with the young impresario Noble Sissle. In 1921, Sissle and Blake produced Broadway's first all-black musical, Shuffle Along. From then

The composing-producing-performing team of Noble Sissle (left) and Eubie Blake (right) ignited the Harlem Renaissance (said poet Langston Hughes) with their wildly successful musical Shuffle Along (1921), which was the first all-black production of its kind.

to World War II, the hits never stopped. After the war, in his sixties, he retired from show business to get a degree in musicology.

Blake lived long enough to be forgotten and rediscovered. In 1978, a successful Broadway musical called Eubie celebrated the then-ninety-five-year-old composer's career, and he received a Presidential Medal of Honor in 1981. James Hubert Blake was one hundred years and five days old when he died in 1983.

Dixieland

Singin' the Blues

The "Mother of the Blues"—Ma Rainey—and her Georgia Jazz Band in 1923, by which time jazz and the blues were inextricably intertwined.

Gertrude "Ma" Rainey (1886–1939), the "Mother of the Blues," said she first heard the blues in 1902. W.C. Handy said he heard them in 1903. And when Jelly Roll Morton made his Library of Congress recordings, one of the songs he sang was "Mamie's Blues," which he said he had learned in New Orleans from the singer Mamie Desdoumes, while he was playing piano in Storyville brothels; that would have been just about the same time—the early 1900s—that Rainey and Handy cited.

Ragtime was a fusion of black and white music, but the blues were black. They evolved deep within black America, in the rural South, out of work songs and spirituals in the decades following the Civil War; indeed, they were what work songs and spirituals became when they turned to issues of love, sex, and everyday survival. The blues were rooted in centuries-old West African traditions of improvisation and call-and-response and in the African scale that came to be called blues tonality.

Singin' the Blues

Unlike ragtime, the blues couldn't be spread via sheet music (although popularized versions like W.C. Handy's could), and their evolution was therefore slower and more organic. By the time they reached the cities, at the turn of the century, they had taken on the classic twelve-bar blues form, but it would be another twenty years—until the birth of recorded music—before that form was as familiar as the adulterated versions were. During those twenty years, the blues worked their way into the heart of the music that was becoming jazz.

But if instrumental jazz and piano ragtime, as they grew, were male provenances, the blues—at least urban blues sung for paying audiences—came to belong to women. Mamie Desdoumes was presumably singing them in the whorehouses of New Orleans about the same time as Ma Rainey was singing them on tour with Rainey's Rabbit Foot Minstrels (William "Pa" Rainey was her husband) early in her career. And once the recordings began—Mamie Smith (1883?–1946) made the first big blues hit with "Crazy Blues," in 1920—it would be women, overwhelmingly, who made them famous, often with great jazz instrumentalists backing them up.

Rainey, for instance—who began recording blues in 1923—sang with Lovie Austin's Blues Serenaders, with the great—and tragically short-lived—Tommy Ladnier (1900–1939) on trumpet. She toured for the entire decade, with a tent that seated fifteen hundred people, often closing her show with an ensemble number called "Ma Rainey's Black Bottom" (which provided the title sixty years later for a successful Broadway musical based on her life and music).

It was Rainey who discovered Bessie Smith, "Empress of the Blues," perhaps the greatest of all blues singers. Smith was touring with Rainey's Minstrels before her eighteenth birthday and later toured with her own show, *Harlem Frolics*. The list of her backup musicians is a "Who's Who" of early jazz.

A dynamic performer in her own right, Rainey was also a skilled manager and generous nurturer of other talents, including Bessie Smith.

Blues singer Victoria Spivey appeared in the first all-black movie-musical, *Hallelujah!* (1929).

Early in the 1920s, the record companies began marketing blues records by black musicians in a special category that was called, frankly enough, "race records" and was aimed at and sold to African American communities exclusively. Scores of women recorded thousands of blues: a short list of the most famous includes, in addition to Rainey and Bessie Smith, Clara Smith (1894–1935), Ida Cox (1889–1967), Victoria Spivey (1906?–1978), Helen Humes (1913–1981), and Sippie Wallace (1899–1986).

It was no accident that the blues caught on in the 1920s. At no earlier time would their frank, earthy lyrics have been allowed in public. Their subject matter covered every aspect of life, from passion and tragedy to the most mundane topics. Bessie Smith sang about bedbugs ("Mean Old Bedbug Blues," 1927); Helen Humes sang about her lover's garlic breath ("Garlic Blues," 1927); and Victoria Spivey sang "T.B. Blues" about tuberculosis.

The most pervasive topic, though, was love—its tribulations and rewards. There were songs about jealousy and desertion, of course; but there were also songs about sex, good and bad. Virtually every woman who recorded the blues sang at least one song in which the singer told the world exactly what she liked and how she liked it, like Ida Cox's "One Hour Mama": "I'm a one-hour mama, so no one-minute papa ain't the kind of man for me."

And the fearless Ma Rainey took plain speaking one step further in "Prove It on Me Blues," with its frankly lesbian lyrics: "Went out last night with a group of my friends, they must have been women, 'cause I don't like no men....It's true I wear a collar and a tie, I like to look at the women as they go by."

Perhaps because of their range and their ability to touch people's—especially black people's—lives so intimately, the blues turned out to be more enduring than ragtime. Influencing every breed of jazz and popular music, they also remained popular in their original form, for their own sake, in both their urban and country varieties.

Through the 1920s and 1930s, a steady trickle of country, or "delta," blues—performed more by men than by women—found their way into the recording studios. In the late 1930s and 1940s the careers of Huddie Ledbetter

Huddie Ledbetter—"Leadbelly" (here with his wife)—sang his way out of two prison sentences and up from poverty. Lou Gehrig's disease (amyotrophic lateral sclerosis) felled him at the age of sixty.

("Leadbelly," 1885–1949) and "Big Bill" Broonzy (1893–1958) captured a wider and more mixed audience than the race records had. By the 1950s, the blues had spawned a whole new genre called rhythm and blues, the basis of rock and roll. The folk music revival of the 1960s triggered interest in the form yet again, and promoters and musicologists searched the South for remaining old-style blues singers like Mississippi John Hurt (1892–1966), Son House (1902–1988), and Skip James (1902–1969). Then, in the 1970s, the feminist movement encouraged new interest in the blues women of the 1920s and 1930s and new respect for their pride and independence.

The blues may turn out to have been the hardiest and most profoundly influential of all American musical genres. They form a chapter in the history of much of today's music, but the story of the blues continues today.

Although he was the best-selling male blues singer of the 1930s, "Big Bill" Broonzy had to supplement his music income by working as a porter and a janitor.

Empress of the Blues: Bessie Smith, 1895?–1937

The blues made Bessie Smith, and she made them. Smith understood the blues at an early age; she and her six siblings were orphaned when Bessie was about seven, and she supported herself by singing on the streets of Chattanooga for pennies.

Smith grew up to be strikingly beautiful, a dark-skinned vocalist of genius circulating at a time when the ideal African American woman performer was the color of "coffee and cream." But she had the luck to be discovered by the "Mother of the Blues," Gertrude "Ma" Rainey. Rainey's Rabbit Foot Minstrels employed *only* dark-skinned women in its chorus line. (Some claimed Rainey didn't want to be surrounded on stage by lighter complexions.)

That was when Bessie was eighteen. She had her own show by 1920. In 1923 she arrived in New York and made her first record, with Columbia, "Downhearted Blues." It sold an astonishing 780,000 copies.

The power and expressiveness of Bessie Smith's voice, still audible on her primitively produced early records, shook listeners as no other blues had. She sang about the range of human experience—about killer floods ("Backwater Blues") and vermin ("Mean Old Bedbug Blues") and every face of love. Her "six-minute masterpiece called 'Empty Bed Blues'" was as moving, said one impressed listener, as an entire Verdi opera.

By 1927, Smith was the highest-paid black performer in the world. She recorded with tenor saxophone genius Coleman Hawkins, bandleader Fletcher Henderson, and—on "St. Louis Blues"—the legendary Louis Armstrong. Touring that year, she sold out shows all across the United States; in Kansas City, one thousand people were turned away from one show.

Bessie Smith enjoyed her success to the hilt, dressing extravagantly (on- and offstage) even for that extravagant era, drinking hard, and loving hard (men and women, it was said). She traveled in a private train, for comfort and to avoid Jim Crow hotels.

Bessie Smith's inimitable blues delivery—as well as her flamboyance—inspired singers from her own time through the rock and roll era.

> By the end of the 1920s, however, sales of blues records were leveling off. Columbia cut no records with Bessie Smith between 1929 and 1933, then produced one last session that included the still-loved nonblues "Gimme a Pigfoot (and a Bottle of Beer)."
>
> She still toured profitably, but not by train. She was being driven from one Mississippi appearance to another the night of September 25, 1937, when her car crashed. They brought her to the Afro-American Hospital in Clarkedale, where she died the next day of loss of blood. She was forty-two years old.
>
> For years after Smith's death, the myth persisted that a nearer white hospital had refused to treat her, but recent research appears to have discredited the story. Bessie's grave remained unmarked until her former housekeeper, Juanita Green, and rock star Janis Joplin—who had modeled her career and her persona on Bessie's—paid for a tombstone more than thirty years later, in 1970. It said, "The greatest blues singer in the world will never stop singing."

Only in New Orleans

Jazz was born in many places, but it was nurtured in New Orleans as nowhere else.

Black, brown, and white musicians met and mingled in New Orleans as they did in no other place in the country. New Orleans, lying at the mouth of the Mississippi, was the terminus for the riverboats that carried brass bands, minstrels, and ragtime around the country. And New Orleans, with its buoyant, anything goes, always-ready-for-a-party soul, had the atmosphere—and the venues—in which the ebullient, improvisational music that was early jazz could flourish.

Those facts are rooted deep in New Orleans' history, all the way back to 1717, when a Scot named John Law began carving a city for the French government out of a malaria- and yellow fever-ridden swampland near the mouth of the Mississippi River. Within little more than a century, in the course of passing from French to Spanish ownership in 1769, back to the French in 1800, and finally, to the young United States in 1803, New Orleans had become "the wickedest city in America."

The city was wide open from the beginning. Even while the mosquito-born diseases were still killing thousands every year, New Orleans was one of the great ports of the New World and the major center of the slave trade.

The rush of trade through New Orleans gave it its permanent inclination to party; prostitution and saloons of every description flourished. And the rush of nations gave it its heterogeneity; it had the most mixed population in the hemisphere, perhaps in the world. In addition to its

Dixieland

French and Spanish families, large numbers of Italians came, along with northern Europeans and, of course—for the first century and a half, involuntarily—Africans.

So rapidly did the African population grow, in fact, that Louisiana was among the first territories to issue a Black Code in 1724. The *Code Noir* regulated every aspect of slaves' lives, banning, for instance, "gatherings" of blacks without a white person present. (There was, however, one licit black "gathering" place, the public space that came to be called Congo Square.) The code also prohibited sexual relations between master and slave, but delineated the procedure by which a master might free a slave and the slave's children, with the blithe—but tacit—understanding that many of those children would be the master's.

By early in the ninteenth century, the three largest ethnic groups in New Orleans were its still-dominant (even after the Louisiana Purchase) French-speaking whites, a substantial number of English-speaking blacks—slave and free—and a large population of people of mixed African and French ancestry. Those of the last group who were free called themselves Creoles of color, spoke a New Orleans dialect of French, and occupied a middle ground in New Orleans' social and economic hierarchy, below the whites but above the slaves and the English-speaking blacks of predominantly African descent who had migrated to New Orleans from elsewhere in the South. Many of the Creoles acquired considerable wealth and even owned slaves themselves; they gave their children European educations when they could and in any case had them trained in European composed music as part of their educations.

Meanwhile, the darker, English-speaking and West Indian immigrant blacks created their own cultural niche in the city. These blacks were much closer to their African roots than were the Creoles of color.

For almost a century, the great Mississippi paddle-wheels carried minstrelsy, ragtime, and finally jazz up and down the river from New Orleans to Iowa and points north.

Some of them still practiced variants of African religions, most prominent among them Voudun, or voodoo. One liberty allowed New Orleans blacks, free or slave, was the freedom to hold once a month dances in Congo Square, where they danced the Calinda, the Bamboula, and other dances of visibly African origin. Many of them, too, maintained the lavish funeral rites that characterize West African cultures.

White New Orleans—which also called itself Creole—still spoke French, thought French, and acted French. Thus, in the Napoleonic Era, when a mania for march music swept France, it swept New Orleans as well; black, brown, and white marching bands became an integral feature of New Orleans. The blacks employed the bands for funerals; the city en masse employed them in the parades—street parties—it threw as often as possible.

The city held a Fourth of July parade as early as 1806. In 1857, it held the first Fat Tuesday—in French, Mardi Gras—parade the day before Ash Wednesday (and so began the history of the other institution for which New Orleans became world famous). The same year, another parade actually scandalized the hard-to-shock city, when New Orleans' huge population of prostitutes danced—some of them naked—through the streets to celebrate a court victory over a repressive law.

The distinctive Spanish-French architecture of "the Quarter" is illustrated by St. Ann Street, French Quarter, New Orleans.

Nor did the massive changes brought about by the Civil War and Emancipation dilute New Orleans' free-living atmosphere or change—at first—its social structure. The combination of freedom and a massive postwar influx of former slaves into the city dissolved some but not all the barriers between Creoles of color and other blacks, but on the whole the Creoles maintained their dominance of the city's population of color until the counter-Reconstructionist policies of the 1870s thrust them all, finally, into the same caste.

Dixieland

The streets of New Orleans have always been music venues as much as routes from one place to another.

In 1874 the White League succeeded in passing new segregation laws in Louisiana. Suddenly, all those with any African ancestry were lumped together legally and with stringent sanctions established for the transgression of "passing" (or attempting to pass) as white. Whites began to refuse to patronize Creole businesses, and the Creoles suffered financially. New Orleans became, basically, a two-tiered city, not a three-tiered one, and—of critical importance in the development of jazz—the classically trained Creoles began to mix, socially and musically, with brass band–trained, river boat–trained, minstrel-trained, and street-trained darker-skinned American blacks.

And they mixed in Storyville.

The legislative establishment of a formal New Orleans red-light district in 1898 stitched the final thread in the jazz tapestry. Prostitution had always flourished in the city; in 1898, the city fathers decided that it would be better to restrict it to one area. So they drew up laws that, while not exactly declaring prostitution legal, forbade it anywhere except the thirty-eight-block district called Storyville.

The laws prohibited black and white prostitutes from working in the same brothel and black customers from patronizing white houses, but it made no distinctions about the race of musicians. Indeed, many people became musicians because they knew they could find work in Storyville, which became the biggest single employer of musicians—black and white—in New Orleans. This continued to be true for almost twenty years, until the United States entered World War I, in 1917, and the federal government objected to the presence of the thriving red-light distinct adjacent to the huge port of New Orleans. Storyville was closed down.

By then, however, Storyville had made its contribution to American musical history. The jazz players who had found their music there moved on, most of them to the north. New Orleans lost its musical primacy, but the music kept its name.

The Trumpet King: Buddy Bolden (1877–1931)

Every jazz player who ever reminisced about the early years in New Orleans talked about Charles Joseph (Buddy) Bolden, whose brief career became a legend and a prototype.

Bolden was prodigious, they said, in every respect: a prodigious drinker, a prodigious dresser, a prodigious womanizer, a cornet player who could be heard ten or twelve miles away. He went mad before he was thirty years old and spent the rest of his life—twenty-four years—in the hospital.

Historians have combed through the records to little avail. What is known is little more than the sum of his contemporaries' recollections.

Buddy was from and of uptown New Orleans (meaning he was African American, not Creole). Born in 1877, he left school at the age of thirteen; a family friend taught him to play the cornet.

In his early teens, Bolden played with Charles Galloway's dance band; it became his own band before he turned twenty-one, although he still had to supplement his music earnings with part-time plastering and the like. He was also a father; he had a child with one Harriet Oliver when he was twenty.

By 1900, his band was playing anywhere and everywhere in New Orleans: in dance halls, cabarets, and saloons—where they were presumably paid—but also on the streets, in parades, and in the parks. Large and handsome, Buddy was a great showman and crowd pleaser. All New Orleans—or at least all black New Orleans—knew the sound of his horn. They called him "King" Bolden.

The performances, however, were accompanied by more and more drinking—and by more and more outrageous and aggressive behavior. During a 1906 parade, he ran amok and was arrested.

In March 1907, he became violent in his own home and attacked his mother, who called the police. They arrested him again. A night in jail failed to sober him up. The next day, he was brought to the Jackson Mental Institute. He remained there until his death in 1931.

One document from his medical history there survives. The record describes him as having auditory and visual hallucinations and gives a diagnosis of "dementia praecox" (the term today is *schizophrenia*).

Buddy Bolden's Band, with the legendary Bolden second from left with his cornet in his hand, in New Orleans (circa 1900).

During his years at Jackson, the Bolden legend grew (and was perhaps embellished). Even before his death, rumored wax cylinders on which the actual sound of his horn was said to have been recorded became a kind of Holy Grail of jazz; historians and collectors have searched for them for over sixty years.

They've never been found.

Dixieland

is it jazz yet? New Orleans, 1900-1917

"Papa" Jack Laine had the most advertising-wagon business. His Reliance Band would pile into a horse-drawn wagon and put a sign on the side advertising a new business or a dance scheduled for that night. Then they would drive around town getting attention for their client with the exuberant new music that added the syncopation of ragtime and the wail of the blues to the old brass-band repertoire of marches, quadrilles, stomps, and polkas.

It was a small band of five or seven pieces. A cornet, trombone, and clarinet played tight ensemble improvisations on popular tunes while a drum, bass, and maybe a banjo hammered out the rhythm. Small as the band was, though, there was

"Papa" Jack Laine (seated) and the Reliance Brass Band in New Orleans (circa 1900).

barely room for all of them in the wagon. The trombone player had to ride tailgate, in the back, facing outward so not to hit the others with his slide and providing the tailgate trombone with a nickname forever more.

Bands like Laine's were putting together the same fusion of sounds all over the country, but the center—the source of it all—was New Orleans. There were hundreds of bands and thousands of musicians: trained, half-trained, and self-taught; black, brown, and white; playing full-time or working at other jobs part-time. They played in New Orleans' dance halls and cabarets, in Lincoln Park and at funerals, and on the riverboats that steamed up from New Orleans and carried the music around the country. Of those thousands of turn-of-the-century players who presided over the birth of jazz, only a handful of bandleaders and bands made it into the annals: the legendary Buddy Bolden; John Robichaux and the Olympia Band; Laine and his Reliance Band; Manuel Perez (1879–1946) and the Onward Brass Band; "Papa" Oscar Celestin (1884–1954) and the Indiana Brass Band; Frankie Dusen (1880?–1940) and his Eagle Band.

Most of them played trumpet or cornet; the trumpet players were the royalty of the nascent jazz scene, and usually led and managed the bands. Bolden—"King" Bolden—played cornet; so did Perez (he also played cello). Celestin played trumpet, and Laine played alto horn (a saxhorn, a member of the trumpet family). (Dusen, a trombone man, was an exception among that company; he took over Bolden's band when Bolden was hospitalized and renamed it the Eagle Band.) Also, the trumpet players faced off in "cutting" contests: street sessions in which two horn men would try to outplay each other. If they were booked into rival establishments for later that night, the winner could count on bigger audiences as well as greater glory.

But the music was not yet called jazz (at least as far as we know now; if anyone ever asked Bolden, Dusen, or Perez just what the name was for what they were doing, no one recorded the answer). Naming the music would be the task of the second generation that was coming up hard on the pioneers' heels, musicians a decade or so younger who within a few short years would carry the music north to Chicago, christen it "jazz," and record it.

Nearly a half century later, that second generation—no longer young—and their immediate successors would supply the jazz historians with the names and stories of those first players. Bolden, Robichaux, Perez, Celestin, Dusen, and Laine may be the best-remembered jazzmen from 1900–1905 not only because of their music, but also because they were the ones who hired and taught the largest number of the players who brought jazz forward.

Dixieland

In the decade that began in 1905, New Orleans was aboil with a staggering roster of talent. They all played around, so to speak, constantly. Bands would form and re-form as musicians were available; many had to keep their day jobs at least part of the time.

Trumpet player Bunk Johnson (William Geary Johnson, 1879–1949) played with Bolden, traveled with McCabe's Minstrels (as did Jelly Roll Morton), and played in bands that were backing up fabled blues singer Mamie Desdoumes in brothels and dance halls. Johnson later taught trumpet to the brilliantly talented and short-lived Tommy Ladnier and still later helped trigger the Dixieland revival and became one of the major chroniclers of the early days in New Orleans.

The Superior Brass Band in 1909, with trumpeter Bunk Johnson (second from left, back row), who would help trigger the Dixieland revival three decades later.

Morton was playing barrelhouse piano in New Orleans dives then and was not among the stellar second-generation jazz players performing nightly in each others' bands; by his later account, he learned about the blues from Mamie Desdoumes. He was at least on the fringes of the jazz milieu, though, and later became a major source of information about Bolden's short career.

The great clarinetist Sidney Bechet (1891–1971) played with Robichaux, with Dusen, and with the Silver Bells Band led by his brother Leonard Bechet (not long afterward, Leonard dropped out of the music business and became a dentist), before he pioneered the Chicago sound and then became an American jazz idol in Paris.

New Orleans, 1900–1917

The incomparable Sidney Bechet.

Trombonist Eddie Edwards (1891–1963) and cornet player Nick LaRocca (1889–1961) played with Laine; they would found the Original Dixieland Jass Band a decade later and thereby name one school of jazz and be the first to record any kind of jazz.

By the end of the period, Fate Marable (1890– 1947) and his riverboat band, the Kentucky Jazz Band, were also employing many of the New Orleans players, including Jelly Roll Morton and the Dodds brothers, clarinetist Johnny (1892–1940) and drummer "Baby" (Warren, 1899–1959).

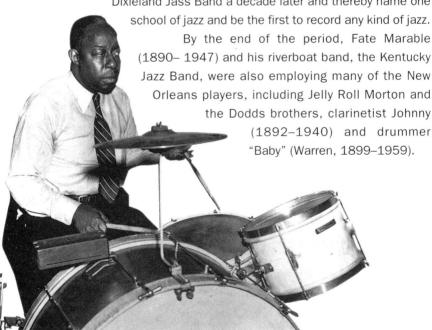

The ubiquitous Warren "Baby" Dodds, greatest drummer of New Orleans–style jazz, played with almost everybody at one time or another.

Dixieland

And everybody played with Frankie Dusen in the Eagle Band: Bechet, Bunk Johnson, banjo player Bill Johnson (1872–1972), and the rising young cornetist Freddie Keppard (1889–1933), who would shortly form his own Olympia Band. Keppard became Buddy Bolden's successor as the most powerful horn player in New Orleans.

Freddie Keppard was to hold the title only briefly, however. A young trumpet player named Joe Oliver (1885–1938)—blind in one eye since his early childhood—was working constantly, with every bandleader who would have him, to get his sound down. He played with Robichaux and

Joe "King" Oliver in New Orleans, 1918.

Like Baby Dodds, trombonist Edward "Kid" Ory played in many Dixieland bands.

Ory also led his own band, the Original Creole Jazz Band.

Perez; he played with Keppard; and he played with trombonist Edward "Kid" Ory (1886–1973). Ory would lead the first all-black band to record jazz a few years later and would have one of the longest-running careers in the business, playing New Orleans–style jazz into the 1960s.

Oliver succeeded. By 1915, he had acquired the title that had lain dormant since Bolden disappeared into the psychiatric hospital at Jackson: Joe Oliver became "King" Oliver. He also became the mentor of the young man who would become the single best-known jazz player—and by some estimates, the greatest trumpet player—in the history of jazz, a youth just out of the Colored Waifs' Home, the incomparable Louis Armstrong (who referred to Oliver as "Papa Joe"). When Oliver led the exodus from New Orleans to Chicago a few years later, there were those who say he was fleeing Armstrong's competition. Whatever the case, Oliver's impact on the development of jazz was enormous, though this fact went unrecognized in his lifetime. Oliver died penniless and toothless in 1938.

Or perhaps the well of New Orleans inspiration was drying up. Before the United States entered World War I, jazz—still nameless—had begun to move beyond the confines of New Orleans. Southern blacks were moving north in record numbers; the 1917 shutdown of Storyville was the final rocking of the jazz cradle. The next center would be Chicago, where jazz would get its name.

Born on the Fourth of July: Louis Armstrong, 1900–1971

Louis Armstrong—"Satchmo"—stands alone, not only in the annals of jazz, but also in the history of American popular culture altogether.

The young Louis Armstrong in 1925.

No other jazz musician ever became as widely known in the world beyond jazz; but then, no other jazz musician had as wide-ranging a career.

Armstrong was a brilliant trumpeter who single-handedly invented jazz singing and had best-selling pop hits as well. He appeared in over two dozen films, making his face as internationally recognizable as his trumpet and his voice. At the peak of his fame, he was probably the best-known and most beloved African American in the world. And from start to finish, his was an American success story—as American as Horatio Alger or the proverbial apple pie.

Whether Armstrong was actually born—as he claimed to have been—on July 4, 1900, is uncertain; he may have fudged the date a little. But he was definitely born in New Orleans, and he was definitely confined to a reform school there at the age of thirteen. He stayed there—in the Colored Waifs' Home—for exactly as long as it took him to learn to play the trumpet.

Then Armstrong was back on the streets of New Orleans, playing his horn and challenging every one of the older trumpet masters, including Freddie Keppard and Joe "King" Oliver. Oliver became his mentor, though he apparently knew early on that his protégé would eclipse him, and in 1919, when Oliver left New Orleans for Chicago, Louis took his place in Kid Ory's band.

In 1922, however, Oliver wrote asking that Armstrong join his Creole Jazz Band in Chicago, and Louis, too, headed north. He would never live in the South again.

The next two years were critical in Armstrong's career. He began recording and was a hit almost at once. His astonishing command of his horn—he was one of the few trumpeters of the time who could regularly hit a high C—was helping to shape the "New Orleans" style of jazz that was coalescing among younger black musicians in Chicago.

But Armstrong was finding it hard to work with Oliver. Most of the members of the band left when they caught Oliver holding out more than his share of his band's proceeds. When Armstrong fell in love with Oliver's extraordinarily talented pianist, Lil Hardin (1898–1971), he decided to make another break. He left before his friendship with Oliver was totally ruined, and they stayed in close touch for the rest of the older man's life.

Louis and Lil married in 1924 and moved to New York, where they played with Fletcher Henderson's band. By the next year, he was leading his own band, Louis Armstrong's Hot Five (sometimes Hot Seven) on OKeh Records. Besides Lil, the band included clarinetist Johnny Dodds and Kid Ory, who had also come up from New Orleans (via

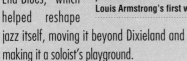
Pianist Lillian Hardin Armstrong, the preeminent woman in early jazz and Louis Armstrong's first wife.

California, where in 1919 he had led the first all-black recording sessions). The 1925 OKeh sessions included Armstrong's first undisputed classic, the great "West End Blues," which helped reshape jazz itself, moving it beyond Dixieland and making it a soloist's playground.

Around this time Armstrong was also developing another major jazz innovation. He began performing the vocals on some of his performances and records, though it was a few more years before he began "scat" singing, which turned the human voice into another jazz instrument.

Louis was on a roll. Nothing stopped his career over the next decades, neither his recurrent lip problems nor his increasingly strained relations with Lil (they divorced in 1938) nor the advent of big band jazz. He formed and re-formed his band, playing steadily and becoming ever more popular.

In 1936 Armstrong made his first appearance on film, with Bing Crosby in *Pennies from Heaven*. The movie role turned out to be the start of still another career: he appeared in twenty-three more movies—always playing himself, more or less—and scored hits in many, like *High Society* (1956) and *Hello, Dolly* (1969). In 1957 Hollywood let him play his real self in *Satchmo the Great*. And from the 1950s on, he had an unbroken string of pop hits, including "Mack the Knife" and "Hello, Dolly."

Though he became far more than a jazz star, Louis never became less of a jazz player. Between the movies and the pop recordings, he continued to play, record, and tour with his own band, which from 1947 on was called—appropriately enough—Louis Armstrong's All Stars. (Its roster included at one point or another trombonist Jack Teagarden [1905–1964], pianist Earl "Fatha" Hines [1903–1983] and clarinetist Barney Bigard [1906–1980].)

In 1959 Louis suffered a heart attack that forced him to cut back what had been, up to that point, a punishing schedule. Not yet ready to retire, he had to admit it was time to slow down.

Louis Armstrong's Hot Five, with Louis on the far left, Lil on the far right.

Armstrong had a big year in 1969, including the movie *Hello, Dolly* and a megahit record of the title song and a triumphal final British tour. The tour, however, may well have cost him the remainder of his health. He died two years later in his home in Queens, New York, on July 6, 1971, just after his seventy-first birthday. He was said to have had a smile on his face.

far from dixie: The Original Dixieland Jazz Bands, 1915-1926

The then-unnamed music that left New Orleans between 1915 and 1919 acquired a name as soon as it arrived in Chicago. Within a few short years—to the eternal confusion of everyone who ever afterward tried to follow the history of jazz—it had three.

"Dixieland jazz" was brought from New Orleans to Chicago in about 1915, named in Chicago by one or two groups of white New Orleans musicians, and first recorded in New York in 1917.

"New Orleans jazz" was a new version of the original New Orleans music refined and named in Chicago by black New Orleans musicians between 1917 and 1924.

"Chicago jazz" was the final flowering of Dixieland/New Orleans in the hands of a group of mostly younger, mostly white, mostly native midwestern musicians between about 1920 and 1926.

Accounts differ about the actual first use of both *Dixieland* and *jazz*, but the first documented appearance of both words dates to Chicago in 1915.

In May 1915 an otherwise-forgettable white band from New Orleans called either "Tom Brown's Band from Dixieland" or "Brown's Dixieland Jass Band" played a summer-long engagement at Lamb's Cafe. They went back on the road in August, without having made much of an impression on Chicago.

Shortly afterward, another white New Orleans group came to Chicago and made a much bigger hit at Schiller's Cafe. In Chicago, it was called "Stein's Dixie Jass Band." Although no record exists, the band had had that name back home in New Orleans; it was led by a New Orleans drummer named Johnny Stein and included at least three alumni of "Papa" Jack Laine's Reliance Band: Nick LaRocca (1889–1961) on cornet, Eddie Edwards (1891–1963) on trombone, and Alcide "Yellow" Nuñez (1884–1934) on clarinet.

They worked around Chicago for almost two years, making personnel changes from time to time. Stein and Nuñez left and were replaced by drummer Tony Spargo (1897–1969) and clarinetist Larry Shields (1899–1953), also from New Orleans.

The Original Dixieland Jazz Bands, 1915–1926

In 1917 the band was booked into Resenweber's restaurant on New York's Columbus Circle. This gig turned out to be a turning point in jazz history. Calling themselves the "Original Dixieland Jass Band" (ODJB), they took New York by storm, and jazz—and Dixieland—were launched.

They stayed on at Resenweber's for months. While there, they made an even more historic debut: the ODJB became the first jazz band to issue a record, putting out definitive early Dixieland sides like "Tiger Rag," "Original Dixieland One-Step," and the jokey novelty number, "Livery Stable Blues."

It was a threshold moment for jazz. Suddenly, anyone and everyone could hear it—and hear it the way its creators played it. Unlike ragtime, which was propagated primarily through sheet music, and the blues, which were put

The Original Dixieland Jazz Band in 1917, the year they arrived in Chicago. From left to right: Henry Ragas, Larry Shields, Eddie Edwards, cofounder Nick LaRocca, and Tony Spargo.

out in their authentic form only by word of mouth (although they were also published in essentially inauthentic forms by composers like W.C. Handy), the real sounds of Dixieland were now available to enormously wider audiences. They were also available to aspiring jazz *players*, a fact that would be critically important in the development of Chicago-style jazz.

The beginning of the recording age was essentially the beginning of real jazz history, as well. From 1917 on, rather than myth-shrouded suppositions about who played what when and what it sounded like, we have the records (not always well-labeled or documented, to be sure, but a major improvement over the wistful and often erroneous memories of Jelly Roll Morton, Bunk Johnson, and their peers).

Dixieland

The New Orleans Rhythm Kings, the most influential of the white Dixieland bands.

In 1919, the ODJB brought Dixieland all the way to London, where music critics panned them viciously—and audiences flocked to hear them. They never returned to Chicago but continued to play, tour, and record until Nick LaRocca collapsed and left the band in 1925 or 1926.

Chicago, though, had got hooked on Dixieland, and in 1921, the Friars Inn asked New Orleans cornetist Paul Mares (1900–1949) to put a group together and bring it to Chicago. The result was the short-lived but musically influential New Orleans Rhythm Kings band.

They were all New Orleans men, including Mares: George Brunis (1900–1974) played trombone, Leon Rappolo (1902–1943) clarinet, Jack Pettis saxophone, Lou Black (1901–1965) banjo, Steve Brown (1890–1965) bass, and Frank Snyder drums. In their own minds, at least, the music they were playing was an imitation of black New Orleans jazz. They were as popular in Chicago as the ODJB had been, and in 1922 they made their first record, with the Gennett Company in nearby Indiana. Within a year, a group of white high school musicians at nearby Austin High School—some of them too young to go to the Friars—were playing the Rhythm Kings' records, especially "Farewell Blues," over and over and over, trying to capture the sound. Ultimately, they would more than capture it; they would accomplish things with it that the Rhythm Kings had never dreamed of.

The next year, in 1923, the Rhythm Kings made the first known racially integrated jazz record when Jelly Roll Morton, who had by then also landed in Chicago, sat in on at least one of their Gennett sessions and recorded with them his own "Milenberg Joys" (named for a suburb back home in New Orleans).

But on the whole, white and black jazz were diverging, not converging. Most of the noted black musicians who had migrated north were creating their own sound on the other side of Chicago, and the Dixieland sound of the Rhythm Kings (they only lasted until 1925) was about to be taken up by a new generation of white musicians.

new orleans north: South Side Chicago, 1917-1924

The great northern migration of African Americans during and after World War I created the Chicago audiences for whom the New Orleans musicians in exile would create the final flowering of "New Orleans" jazz.

Not that white Chicago opened its arms to the new arrivals. Between 1917 and 1921, at least fifty-eight black homes were bombed. In 1919 a white police officer refused to arrest a white man who had killed a black youth, setting off a four-day race riot that killed almost fifty, about two-thirds of them black. But the city had jobs—some jobs, anyway—and the rural South had none, and the migration continued and was reflected in the movements of artists and especially of musicians.

King Oliver wasn't the first to arrive in Chicago; the great saxophonist Sidney Bechet had preceded him by a year or two. But Oliver's 1919 arrival would bring literally scores of his colleagues along in short

King Oliver's Creole Band in San Francisco, 1921, before Armstrong joined the band. Oliver is playing trumpet (third from left) next to Lil Hardin (center).

Dixieland

order. Oliver went to work immediately with Laurence Duhé's New Orleans Jazz Band but within a year had formed his own Original Creole Jazz Band. By 1920 and the beginning of Prohibition, one bystander counted no fewer than forty important New Orleans players working in Chicago.

Prohibition in Chicago created more work for musicians, not less. Employment abounded for limitless numbers, black and white, in the mob-run "cafes," dance halls, and "gardens." For a short time, Bechet and Oliver both worked at the Dreamland Cafe; Bechet also played at the Deluxe Cafe, as did Freddie Keppard; Jelly Roll Morton and pianist Earl (later "Fatha") Hines both played at the Elite No. 2. Clarinetist Johnny Dodds and his unruly younger brother, the drummer Warren. "Baby" Dodds, and their New Orleans Wanderers played for a long time at Kelly's Livery Stable.

By 1922, when Oliver sent for Louis Armstrong, the Creole Jazz Band was semipermanently ensconced at Lincoln Gardens and consisted almost entirely of New Orleans musicians. Both Dodds brothers were playing in it, as were trombonist Honoré Dutry (who would later lead his own Lincoln Gardens band until his untimely death at thirty-nine from lung damage sustained in the navy) and drummer Bill Johnson. Pianist Lil Hardin stood out, not only as a woman in an otherwise all-male band, but also as the only band member who hadn't been born in New Orleans.

Earl "Fatha" Hines (left) played piano with Armstrong in the 1920s; Texas trombonist Jack Teagarden (right) was called the best white blues singer in early jazz.

There was constant personnel swapping among the bands, with one night's bandleader being the next week's sideman in another group. They were learning to play a smoother, more polished jazz than they had played back home in New Orleans (years later one colleague said, wistfully, that Oliver in particular had lost in drive what he gained in polish). The bands were getting larger and saxophones were incorporated for the first time.

The most profound change, however, was the technological one: the explosive growth of the recording industry and the astonishing numbers of records jazz players were producing all across the country. Johnny Dodds, to name only one, produced forty numbers on five different labels with the

South Side Chicago, 1917–1924

King Oliver's stellar Creole Jazz Band of 1923, with (from left to right) Johnny and Baby Dodds, Honoré Dutry, Armstrong, Oliver, Hardin, and Bill Johnson.

Oliver band alone during this period. Jelly Roll Morton was in his prime as well, producing his most classic recordings with his own Red Hot Peppers on the Gennett label.

The Original Creole Jazz Band collapsed in 1924, when the Dodds found out that Oliver was holding out money on band members. When Armstrong and Hardin left for New York, Oliver put together a new band, the Dixie Syncopaters. It included saxophone players Barney Bigard and Albert Nicholas—also New Orleans men—and the doomed trumpet player Tommy Ladnier.

The next year, the Dixie Syncopaters went to New York, but Oliver was unable to attain the leading position there he had held in Chicago. He was on a downward slide. The bookings and recording sessions diminished, and dental problems—the trumpeter's bane—were destroying his sound. By 1936 he was unable to play and drifted to Savannah, Georgia, where he became a janitor in a poolroom; he died there in 1938.

The collapse of the Creole Jazz Band in 1924 had signaled—though no one could have known it then—the end of the brief flowering of New Orleans jazz in Chicago. Sidney Bechet had already left for New York. (From there he went to Europe, where he became France's resident larger-than-life American jazzman, a position he held for the rest of his life).

The New Orleans jazz players were scattering, drawn by even bigger audiences in New York and lured by the new, bigger bands. The New Orleans sound would be succeeded in Chicago by one last generation of Dixie-descended jazz, the Chicago sound of a group of young white Chicago musicians.

Sidney Bechet (center), here playing clarinet, was the only prominent New Orleans jazzman to play soprano sax.

Jazz, Chicago-Style: 1922-1928

On the South Side of Chicago in 1921, the fourteen-year-old "Muggsy" Spanier (Francis Joseph Spanier, 1906–1967) would sneak into cabarets to listen to King Oliver play. In a Chicago suburb in 1924, the teenaged would-be musicians who became known as the Austin High School Gang would sit around afternoons playing the New Orleans Rhythm Kings' records and trying to copy their licks. And about the same time, Bix Beiderbecke (1903–1931), the Midwest's first jazz genius, was recording the first homegrown Midwest jazz.

Native Chicagoan Francis "Muggsy" Spanier later brought the original Chicago sound to the Dixieland revival.

All those phenomena would eventually contribute to the evolution of Chicago-style jazz. But, unlike the New Orleans sound, Chicago jazz was actually three separate jazz trends. One set of young, white musicians attached themselves to New Orleans jazz; one set followed Dixieland; and the third set synthesized elements of each of the other two.

Younger musicians flocked around King Oliver virtually as soon as he arrived in Chicago, as they had in New Orleans. Muggsy Spanier's pursuit of Oliver's sound—and later of Armstrong's—would make a great jazz trumpeter out of him. But Spanier wasn't the only Chicago kid looking for jazz.

Jazz, Chicago-Style: 1922–1928

Milton "Mezz" Mezzrow, who was an advocate of marijuana use and a major proponent of black culture, on fabled Fifty-second Street (circa 1945).

There was also the young clarinetist Mezz Mezzrow (Milton Mesirow, 1899–1972), who even in the irony-laden history of jazz was a special case. Mezzrow was in love, not only with black jazz, but also with all things African. A few years later, he would carry his version of Chicago jazz to New York City, move to Harlem, and spend the rest of his career playing and recording a kind of neo–New Orleans jazz with black musicians, usually as the only white player in the band. (He was also one of the first musicians to make a virtual sacrament out of the use of marijuana, a sacrament he took—and proselytized—frequently. He always carried a shoebox full, and supplied most of his colleagues, including, it was said, Louis Armstrong.) Though Mezzrow's passion for marijuana and black culture made him a figure of fun to some musicians and commentators, the sessions he recorded in New York in the late 1930s (including "Comin' On With the Come-On" and "Really the Blues") with Sidney Bechet and the terminally ill Tommy Ladnier are widely thought to be among the treasures of late New Orleans/Chicago jazz. He ended up in Paris along with Bechet, living among French jazzophiles and writing, in his autobiography and elsewhere, about the glories of jazz, Harlem and marijuana in the 1920s and 1930s.

Dixieland

Two even younger aspiring Chicago musicians who hung out around Oliver and the other New Orleans exiles were clarinet player Benny Goodman (1909–1986) and drummer Gene Krupa (1909–1973). They ended up playing not Chicago jazz, but big band swing, to which they brought lessons and techniques they learned at Oliver's knee.

The youngsters came from farther afield than Chicago, too. Guitar and banjo player Eddie Condon (1905–1973) arrived from Indiana a couple of years later, stayed long enough to record the first sessions of "official" Chicago jazz in 1927, and then left for New York and worked from there the rest of his life. He opened his own club on New York's fabled Fifty-second Street, broadcast over radio and television, probably wrote more about Chicago jazz than any other player, and recorded with virtually every major jazz player who ever set foot in New York, including Armstrong and a host of lesser luminaries like Texas trombonist Jack Teagarden (1904–1964, known as the only white man who could really sing the blues), cornet player Wild Bill Davison (1906–1989), and most of the alumni of the Austin High School gang.

The account of the kids from Austin High may in one sense be the simplest in the annals of jazz: a bunch of white kids sitting around listening to the music learn it and grow up—virtually all of them—to be players and shapers of jazz.

Yet their collective careers also encapsulate all the changes jazz ever went through. The most profound change reflected by the Austin High story is the difference wrought by the effect the budding record industry had on the mode of transmission of jazz from generation to generation.

The Austin High Gang was the youngest group of Dixieland innovators. From left to right: Frank Teschemacher, Jim Lannigan, Bud Freeman, Jimmy McPartland, Dave Tough, Floyd O'Brien, Dave North, and Dick McPartland.

Jazz, Chicago-Style: 1922–1928

A New York club owner and a raconteur with an inexhaustible fund of stories, Eddie Condon (with banjo) later helped keep traditional jazz alive.

In 1923 the New Orleans Rhythm Kings had just released their first records. Just outside Chicago, in a suburb called Austin, a young high-school saxophone player named Bud Freeman (1906–1991) got hold of one of the records and was—as he might have said years later—blown away. He had never heard anything like it.

So Freeman played it for some friends, and then they tried to get some more musicians together. Eventually, Freeman and cornet player Jimmy McPartland; Jimmy's brother Dick (1905–1957), who played banjo; clarinetist Frank Teschemacher (1906–1932); tuba player Jim Lanigan; drummer Dave Tough (1908–1948); and piano player Dave North would play the recording of the Rhythm Kings' "Farewell Blues" until the grooves wore down, listening to and then playing one phrase after another. This was the first time in the twenty-five-year history of jazz that its improvisations had been passed along not by one musician sitting in with others in a kind of give and take, but by apprentices a world away from the masters (who themselves had been imitating the original New Orleans masters they had sat in with).

When the Austin High kids felt they had learned enough, they called themselves Blue Friars (perhaps in honor of the Friars Inn, where the Rhythm Kings had played when they first came to town) and went to work as a band. They were playing what they thought was Dixieland, but wasn't. They had reconstituted Dixieland; they were playing one strain of Chicago-style jazz. They were performing with Eddie Condon by 1928 and all over the country not long afterward.

Then there was Bix (Leon Bix Beiderbecke, 1903–1931), who in his brief but extraordinarily influential encounter with Chicago-style jazz single-handedly spun its third strand. Beiderbecke, who was a story unto himself, was well on his way to creating a truly modern music when he drank himself to death at the age of twenty-eight.

The mainstream of jazz had long since drifted past Chicago, Dixieland, and New Orleans styles and into the era of swing and the big

Dixieland

Future big band leader Tommy Dorsey (right) played with an early Bix Beiderbecke (second from right) band.

band. Many musicians still played one or another variety of traditional jazz—Bechet and Mezzrow in New York and Europe, Condon in New York, Armstrong anywhere he was, to name a few. But it seemed as if their music would fade away as they did.

Instead, it received an infusion of new energy about a decade after it began to ebb, an infusion that came to be called the Dixieland Revival.

Odd Band Out: McKinney's Cotton Pickers

While young Benny Goodman was listening to King Oliver and Louis Armstrong in the mid-1920s, another black jazz band was performing around the Midwest that was playing neither Dixieland nor any Chicago variation thereof. Along with Fletcher Henderson (1897–1952) in New York, the Detroit-based McKinney's Cotton Pickers was pioneering the kind of jazz that ten years later would sweep the country as big band swing, with Goodman as its king.

In Detroit, the French-born Jean Goldkette (1899–1962) was operating several bands out of the Greystone Ballroom. By 1924, Goldkette's organization was the best place in the country for a jazz-oriented dance band. So it was there that the drummer Bill McKinney (1895–1969) brought the Synco Jazz Band as soon as he became its manager.

McKinney had played drums with the Synco Jazz Band, an ensemble from Springfield, Ohio, since sometime after World War I. When he moved it to Detroit, he changed its name to McKinney's Cotton Pickers and went to work for Goldkette. In 1927, he took the third step that would make McKinney's the most popular band in the Midwest (and the most important one in the country, outside of Chicago and New York): he hired saxophone player Don Redman (1900–1964) away from Fletcher Henderson as his musical director.

McKinney's band was recording from 1924 on, and on its surviving records is some of the most highly regarded early big band music. Their fine version of Jelly Roll Morton's "Milenberg Joys" is a classic. Unfortunately, it is unclear today which of the recordings was actually recorded by McKinney's band, since some that are credited to them were actually Goldkette's; some with Goldkette's name were actually made by McKinney's Cotton Pickers; and some were recorded under Redman's leadership and the name Chocolate Dandies.

Over the next several years, McKinney and Redman (separately) played with some of the stellar names of 1920s jazz. The tenor jazz giant Coleman Hawkins (1904–1969), the great alto saxophonist Benny Carter (b. 1907), the incomparable pianist Fats Waller (1904–1943), and the cornet player Rex Stewart (1907–1967) all played at least once with the McKinney band.

The Cotton Pickers split up and reformed more than once between 1930 and 1940, the year McKinney last led a band. Redman left the band in 1931 and eventually became the only black bandleader in the country with his own radio show. Later, Redman arranged music for major bands, including Duke Ellington's.

When big bands became the major force in American popular music in the 1930s, the big sellers where white bands (though Goodman's was always integrated). But the influence of McKinney's Cotton Pickers and its alumni on that music can hardly be overstated; Don Redman alone, says one commentator, "did as much as anyone to bring about the Swing Era."

McKinney's Cotton Pickers at the Arcadia Ballroom, Detroit, before Don Redman joined the band. Cuba Austin is on drums; Bill McKinney is third from right.

Dixieland

Young Man with a Horn: Bix Beiderbecke, 1903–1931

Bix Beiderbecke came from Davenport, Iowa, a child of middle America. Davenport is on the Mississippi, just across the river from Rock Island, Illinois, and the riverboats came all the way up, bearing the music from New Orleans.

Beiderbecke taught himself to play piano as a child; then when he was fifteen, he taught himself the cornet. By that time, he had heard the records of the Original Dixieland Jazz Band and had heard Armstrong himself, live, playing in Fate Marable's riverboat band.

By 1923, barely twenty, Beiderbecke was playing lead cornet with a band called the Wolverines, often considered the first real Chicago-style band. In Chicago, with his friend and colleague saxophone player Frank Trumbauer (1901–1956), Bix sat in with Oliver and Armstrong and infused the embryonic new style with some of his own lyricism.

But Bix was headed in another direction, figuratively and literally. Over the next several years he took jobs with a series of big bands, including the father of all big bands, the Paul Whiteman Orchestra. He was also composing impressionistic piano pieces that were half jazz, half something more like the music of such European composers as Debussy. "In a Mist," his most famous solo piano recording, looked forward generations ahead of Chicago-style jazz to something more modern than bebop.

In 1927 Beiderbecke's uncontrolled drinking began to take a toll on his health—and on his ability to fulfill his engagements. Repeatedly, his employers and his friends forgave him his excesses, though he might have been better off had they not. In 1931 he had his last bout with pneumonia, then, as now, the alcoholic's bane (though back then it was incurable). If he had obeyed his doctors' orders, he might still have survived; he was only twenty-eight and presumably still had some physical resilience.

But Beiderbecke had never obeyed anybody's wishes and wasn't

Frankie Trumbauer (seated, fourth from left) was Bix Beiderbecke's (standing, second from left) most important collaborator.

about to start. The young man collapsed and died in New York and was brought home to Davenport for burial.

Bix Beiderbecke became one of the great cult figures of early jazz. In the 1930s the whole jazz world recognized the Bix-like protagonist of Dorothy Baker's novel, *Young Man with a Horn*, which was filmed in 1950 and starred Kirk Douglas as the trumpet player.

Beiderbecke is alone among the jazz players of his time in that his music has been continuously available—all his recordings remain in print today.

When he played the cornet, Bix was a brilliant innovator of traditional jazz, but his piano music reached further yet, drawing its inspiration from the works of the French composer Claude Debussy.

still going: The Dixieland Revival, 1942-1995

The Dixieland Revival can fairly be said to have begun with Bunk Johnson's new teeth in 1942.

A country at war was listening to big band music, and traditional jazz was a backwater, a museum piece. Most of the first jazz players were gone. Buddy Bolden had died over a decade before in a Louisiana madhouse (the same year Bix Beiderbecke burned out his scarcely flowered genius). Freddie Keppard of the Eagle Band had died in 1933; King Oliver had died a janitor in 1938; Frankie Dusen, who had taken over leadership of Bolden's band, had died in 1940, as had the straitlaced Johnny Dodds. (His unruly brother "Baby" Dodds was still alive and playing.)

Dixieland

Louis Armstrong (left) watches as Bunk Johnson plays the trumpet again, new teeth in place. It was Johnson's new teeth that triggered the Dixieland revival.

"I thought I heard Buddy Bolden say ...," Jelly Roll Morton had sung in "Buddy Bolden's Blues" for the Library of Congress in 1938, "I thought I heard Frankie Dusen shout...." Then Morton himself died in California in 1941.

Of the survivors, few were still playing. "Papa" Jack Laine, almost seventy, had long since retired; so had "Papa" Celestin, though he was not yet sixty. Nick LaRocca of the Original Dixieland Jazz Band had drifted away from music while still in his forties. Tooth trouble had left Bunk Johnson, who had played with Buddy Bolden, doing odd jobs in Louisiana.

Louis Armstrong was leading a big band. Fletcher Henderson, who had brought Louis into his own band at the start of the big band era, was arranging for the King of Swing, Benny Goodman (who had started his career listening to Armstrong and Oliver in Chicago in the early 1920s).

Kid Ory had come out of retirement a couple of years before; though there was virtually no one left with whom he could play the original jazz that had sprung up on the streets of New Orleans forty years before, a handful of traditionalists were still playing its New Orleans and Chicago versions. Ory played for a while with Sidney Bechet—now playing soprano saxophone as well as clarinet—who only a couple of years earlier had recorded some of the most highly regarded New Orleans sessions ever with Mezz Mezzrow and Tommy Ladnier. (Bechet's brother Leonard had long since left music for dentistry, a career choice that turned out to be not insignificant in the history of jazz.) In New York, Eddie Condon was keeping Chicago style alive with the help of other old-timers like clarinetist Pee Wee Russell (1906–1969) and Wild Bill Davison (1906–1989).

That was the traditional jazz scene in 1942, when two jazz historians, Frederick Ramsey and William Russell, achieved something they thought was necessary to re-create the jazz sound of forty years before: they supplied a new set of teeth for Bunk Johnson.

The Dixieland Revival, 1942–1955

Ramsey and Russell had seen Johnson's name in accounts of the early bands (he had never recorded) and tracked him down. He persuaded the historians that, if only he had teeth, he'd be able to play them the real thing. Jazz players and jazz fans around the country contributed to a Bunk Johnson tooth fund. Leonard Bechet created the teeth.

Johnson put together a band in New Orleans that included another previously unrecorded New Orleans player, clarinetist George Lewis (1900–1968), and the still-rowdy Baby Dodds, and they proceeded to record over one hundred sides of what critics described as "pure" jazz.

Ramsey and Russell wrote their book *Jazzmen*; more significantly, the Dixieland revival was on.

Suddenly, there was work for everybody. Bechet and Mezzrow formed one band after another, sometimes together, sometimes apart, winding up by the 1950s in Europe. Condon opened his own club in 1946 and kept Pee Wee Russell and Wild Bill Davison working for the rest of their lives. Louis Armstrong went back to small-band New Orleans jazz; Jack Teagarden played with him for a while.

New, young musicians began taking up traditional jazz as well, keeping the music alive to pass on to future generations (although, curiously, just as the early jazz players were finally reintegrating—most of the bands were racially mixed at this point—virtually all of the neo-Dixielanders were white).

In 1949 two brothers from New Orleans, Frank (1922–1974) and Fred (1929–1966) Assunto, the sons of New Orleans banjo and trombone player Jacob "Papa Jac" Assunto (1905–1985), founded the Dukes of Dixieland, which lasted through the 1950s. They were enough of a success that Armstrong cut a couple of records with them at the end of the decade.

The founding trio of the Dukes of Dixieland, from left to right: Native New Orleanians Fred, Frank, and "Papa Jac" Assunto.

Dixieland

The Firehouse Five + 2, formed in Los Angeles the same year as the Dukes of Dixieland, were a decidedly untraditional mixture of Hollywood and New Orleans jazz. Amateur musicians and proud of it, they tried to create the impression of being a bunch of firefighters playing jazz in their spare time (several of them actually worked for movie studios). But the band recorded for twenty years and at one point managed to enlist a Kid Ory veteran, soprano sax player George Arthur Probert, Jr. (b. 1927).

Perhaps the most successful Dixieland revivalists have been New Orleans trumpet player Al Hirt (Alois Maxwell Hirt, b. 1922) and clarinetist Pete Fountain (b. 1930). They have played neo-Dixieland together and separately since 1960, although Hirt has worked in a wider range of genres; Fountain has limited himself more to traditional music.

There is also the Dirty Dozen Brass Band, which plays a kind of evolutionary Dixieland. All but one of the young musicians—all born since 1950—who started it in 1977 are from New Orleans, and two are second-

The Dukes of Dixieland in the 1950s, with the Assuntos in the center.

The Dixieland Revival, 1942–1955

Trumpeter Al Hirt in 1970.

generation traditional players. Trombonist Charles Lee Joseph (1954–) and sousaphonist Kirk Matthew Joseph (1961–) are the sons of New Orleans trombonist Waldron "Frog" Joseph. They describe what they play as "jazz gumbo."

Finally, the city of New Orleans itself goes to some lengths to see that the original beat goes on there. It has held a New Orleans Jazz Festival (featuring several kinds of music) every year since 1970 and maintains Preservation Hall on St. Peter Street as a living repository of traditional jazz.

The lost birth certificate for Dixieland jazz might well have shown 1995 as its centennial. The music that came together so organically and joyously in and around New Orleans lasted in its original, "pure" form for perhaps twenty years. Its continuations and revival have been going on for eighty. It looks as if—like rock and roll—Dixieland will never die.

Pete Fountain appearing on the *Lawrence Welk Show* in 1958.

coda: beyond dixie— Big Bands, Boogie-Woogie, Bebop

The century-old music that Buddy Bolden and his peers blasted out of the streets of New Orleans has passed through metamorphosis after metamorphosis ever since. Not every change meant the end of a previous style; new forms have arisen while old ones retained their basic character.

The result has been a steady increase in the forms of jazz. Among the most prominent, over the decades, have been the big band music of the 1930s and 1940s, the boogie-woogie piano music of the same time, and standing alone at a crossroads of jazz in the 1940s, bebop.

By the end of the 1920s, jazz had become swollen with success. Paul Whiteman (1890–1967) had drawn larger, whiter audiences to larger, whiter bands, but at the expense of what had seemed to be the very heart of jazz: improvisation. Spontaneity was all but lost as the big bands of the 1930s—Whiteman's, Benny Goodman's, the Dorsey Brothers'—returned to orchestrated and controlled ensemble playing.

Most of the white-led big bands were for the most part all-white, though Goodman's was always an exception. It was the black big bands, like Fletcher Henderson's and Count Basie's, that kept many of the older jazz players working. And for decades, Duke Ellington (1899–1974), the giant of African American big band music, continued to create innovative expressions of orchestrated jazz.

During the same period, one form of jazz went in the opposite direction. Solo pianists developed a barroom style of blues- and ragtime-influenced playing that came out of the Louisiana lumber camps as boogie-woogie. The first record that bore that name was "Pine Top's Boogie Woogie," recorded in 1928 by Pine Top (Clarence) Smith (1904–1929) but not released until several years after his death. It touched off a fad, spurred on by Tommy Dorsey's 1938 big band version. Other boogie-woogie pianists, like Meade Lux Lewis (1905–1964) and Albert Ammons (1907–1949), who had been eking out their piano earnings with other jobs, reaped some benefits.

Then, in the early 1940s, the most profound transformation in jazz since its inception was born when a group of young, African American musical revolutionaries in New York began improvising around chords instead of melodies. The innovators—most renowned among them Charlie "Yardbird" Parker (1920–1955), Dizzy Gillespie (1917–1993), Thelonious Monk (1917–1982), and Charles Mingus (1922–1979), and Miles Davis (1926–1991)—called it bebop, rebop, or just bop, and it would be the progenitor of every subsequent movement in jazz.

Bebop would hardly have been recognizable as jazz to Buddy Bolden. Yet it remains the heir—or perhaps, by now, jazz is the heirs, in the plural—to the musical legacy of Bolden and Jelly Roll Morton and King Oliver and Louis Armstrong. And wherever jazz is performed, its players are still elaborating on the themes—no matter how distant—established over a century ago in the creation of the first music America could call its own.

At a jam session in 1948, two of the greatest jazz innovators of all time play side by side: bebop saxophone legend Charlie Parker and modern trumpet genius Miles Davis.

BIBLIOGRAPHY

Arnaud, Gérald, and Jacques Chesnel. *Masters of Jazz*. New York/Edinburgh: W & R Chambers, 1991.

Berendt, Joachim E. *The Jazz Book*, 6th ed. Rev. by Günther Huesman. Brooklyn, N.Y.: Lawrence Hill Books, 1992.

Brooks, Tilford. *America's Black Musical Heritage*. Englewood Cliffs, N.J.: Prentice Hall, 1984.

Carr, Ian, Digby Fairweather, and Brian Priestley. *Jazz: The Essential Companion*. New York: Prentice Hall Press, 1988.

Chase, Gilbert. *America's Music*. Rev. 3d ed. Urbana/Chicago: University of Illinois Press, 1987.

Chilton, John. *Who's Who of Jazz*, 4th ed. New York: DaCapo Press, 1985.

Claghorn, Charles E. *Biographical Dictionary of Jazz*. Englewood Cliffs, N.J.: Prentice Hall, 1982.

Clarke, Donald, ed. *The Penguin Encyclopedia of Popular Music*. London: Penguin Books, Ltd., 1990.

Clayton, Peter, and Peter Gammond. *The Guinness Jazz A–N*. London: Guinness Superlatives Ltd., 1986.

Feather, Leonard. *The Encyclopedia of Jazz*. New York: Horizon Press, 1960.

Lyons, Len, and Don Perlo. *Jazz Portraits*. New York: Quill Books (William Morrow), 1989.

McRae, Barry. *The Jazz Handbook*. Boston: G.K. Hall & Co., 1989.

Ostransky, Leroy. *Jazz City*. Englewood Cliffs, N.J.: Prentice Hall, 1978.

Placksin, Sally. *American Women in Jazz*. Wideview Books, 1982.

Schuller, Gunther. *Early Jazz: Its Roots and Musical Development.* New York: Oxford University Press, 1968.

Stearns, Marshall. *The Story of Jazz.* London/Oxford/New York: Oxford University Press, 1956.

SUGGESTED READING

Albertson, Chris. *Bessie.* New York: Stein and Day, 1972.

Armstrong, Louis. *Satchmo: My Life in New Orleans.* New York: Da Capo, 1986.

Berry, Jason, Jonathan Foose, and Tad Jones. *Up from the Cradle of Jazz: New Orleans Music Since World War II.* Athens, Ga.: University of Georgia Press, 1986.

Chilton, John. *Sidney Bechet: The Wizard of Jazz.* New York: Oxford University Press, 1987.

Lomax, Alan. *Mr. Jelly Roll.* Berkeley, Calif.: University of California Press, 1973.

Mezzrow, Milton "Mezz," and Bernard Wolfe. *Really the Blues.* Garden City, N.Y.: Random House, 1946.

Ramsey, Frederic, and Charles E. Smith, eds. *Jazzmen.* New York: Limelight, 1985.

Shapiro, Nat, and Nat Hentoff. *Hear Me Talkin' to Ya.* New York: Dover, 1966.

Sudhalter, Richard, and Philip R. Evans. *Bix: Man and Legend.* New Rochelle, N.Y.: Arlington House, 1974.

Wolfe, George C. *Jelly's Last Jam.* Theatre Commission, 1993.

Dixieland

SUGGESTED LISTENING

Armstrong, Louis. *The Louis Armstrong Story* (Columbia).

Bechet, Sidney, and Mezz Mezzrow. *The King Jazz Story* (Storyville). (Note: King Jazz was Bechet and Mezzrow's own label, briefly.)

Bechet, Sidney, et al. *The Young Bechet* (Jazz Archives).

Beiderbecke, Bix. *The Bix Beiderbecke Story* (Columbia).

Condon, Eddie. *Dixieland Jam* (Columbia).

History of Classic Jazz, Vol. 4: New Orleans Style (Riverside).

Joplin, Scott. *Piano Rags by Scott Joplin*, played by Joshua Rifkin (Nonesuch).

McKinney's Cotton Pickers. *McKinney's Cotton Pickers (1928–1930): The Band Don Redman Built* (Bluebird).

Morton, Jelly Roll. *New Orleans Memories* (Atlantic).

Oliver, Joseph King. *King Oliver's Jazz Band, 1923–26* (Classics). (Note: playing with Oliver on one or another cut on this record are Louis Armstrong, Johnny and Baby Dodds, Jelly Roll Morton, and Kid Ory, among others.)

The Original Dixieland Jazz Band. *The Original Dixieland Jazz Band* (ASB Living Era).

Ory, Edward "Kid." *KID ORY 1944–46* (American Music). (Note: Leadbelly plays on this record.)

Rainey, Ma. *Ma Rainey* (Milestone).

Smith, Bessie. *The Bessie Smith Story* (Columbia).

Spanier, Muggsy. *Muggsy Spanier at Club Hangover* (Storyville).

Teagarden, Jack. *King of the Blues Trombone* (Columbia).

PHOTOGRAPHY CREDITS

ARCHIVE PHOTOS: 37
Archive Photos/Frank Driggs Collection: 8, 23, 25 (B), 31, 38, 39 (T)
ART RESOURCE:
© National Museum of American Art, Washington, D.C./Art Resource, NY (#1967-59-1080): 12
BETTMANN NEWSPHOTOS:
The Bettmann Archive: 14, 35 (B), 45 (B)
UPI/Bettmann: 20, 57 (T)
LEO DE WYS:
© Chuck Fishman/Leo De Wys: 30

FRANK DRIGGS COLLECTION: 2, 22, 24 (T), 26, 32, 34, 35 (T), 36 (T), 41, 43, 45 (T), 46, 47, 48, 51, 52, 53, 54, 56
EVERETT COLLECTION: 55
FPG: 44
© McDaniels/FPG: 29
GLOBE PHOTOS: 13, 36 (B)
NORTHWIND PICTURE ARCHIVE: 11
NEAL PETERS COLLECTION: 39 (B)
The Lester Glassner Collection: 15, 21, 49
PHOTOFEST: 17, 57 (B)

RETNA:
© David Redfern/Retna Ltd.: 7
© Max Jones Files/Redfern/Retna: 28, 42, 50
© William Gottlieb/Retna: 59
SUPERSTOCK:
"RAGTIME" by Albert Bloch/Superstock: 19
Key: T = Top, B = Bottom
FRONT JACKET
Background: © Donovan Reese/Tony Stone Images;
© Everett Collection:
Armstrong and Beiderbecke;
© Archive Photos: band;
© Superstock: riverboat

INDEX

African slaves, importation of, 12
Ammons, Albert, 58
Armstrong, Louis, 26, 37, 38–39, *38*, 44, 45, *45*, 47, 48, 50, 52, 54, *54*, 55
Assunto, Frank, 55, *55*, 56
Assunto, Fred, 55, *55*, 56
Assunto, Jacob "Papa Jac," 55, *55*, 56
Austin, Cuba, *51*
Austin High School Gang, 46, 48, 49

Bechet, Leonard, 34, 54, 55
Bechet, Sidney, 34, *35*, 36, 43, 44, 45, *45*, 47, 50, 54, 55
Beiderbecke, Leon Bix, 46, 49, *50*, 52–53
Berlin, Irving, 19
Bigard, Barney, 39, 45
Blake, Eubie, 18, 20–21
Blake, James Hubert. See Blake, Eubie.
Bolden, Buddy, 31, 33, 53, 54

Bolden, Charles Joseph. See Bolden, Buddy.
Broonzy, "Big Bill," 25, *25*

Cantor, Eddie, 16
Carter, Benny, 51
Celestin, "Papa" Oscar, 33, 54
Chauvin, Louis, 18
Chicago jazz, 40, 41, 46
Condon, Eddie, 48, 49, *49*, 50, 54, 55
Cox, Ida, 24

Davis, Miles, 59, *59*
Davison, Wild Bill, 48, 54, 55
Debussy, Claude, 19–20, 53
Desdoumes, Mamie, 9, 22, 23, 34
Dirty Dozen Brass Band, 56
Dixieland jazz, 7, 19, 40, 46, 57
Dixieland Revival, 34, 50, 53
Dodds, Johnny, 35, 38, 44–45, *45*, 53
Dodds, Warren "Baby," 35, *35*, 44, 45, *45*, 53, 55
Dorsey, Tommy, *50*, 58
Dukes of Dixieland, 55, *55*, 56

Dusen, Frankie, 33, 36, 53
Dutry, Honoré, 44, *45*

Eagle Band, 33, 36
Edwards, Eddie, 35, 40, *41*
Ellington, Duke, 58
"The Entertainer," 20, 21

Firehouse Five + 2, 56
Foster, Stephen, 15
Fountain, Pete, 56, *57*
Freeman, Bud, *48,* 49
Funeral, New Orleans jazz, 13, 29

Gillespie, Dizzy, 59
Goldkette, Jean, 50, 51
Goodman, Benny, 48, 50, 54, 58

Handy, William Christopher, 6, 16–17, 22, 23, 41
Hardin, Lil, 38, 39, *39, 43,* 44, 45, *45*
Hawkins, Coleman, 26, 51
Henderson, Fletcher, 26, 50, 54, 58
Hines, Earl "Fatha," 39, 44, *44*
Hirt, Alois Maxwell, 56, *57*
House, Son, 25

Dixieland

Humes, Helen, 24
Hurt, John, 25

James, Skip, 25
Johnson, Bill, 36, 44, *45*
Johnson, Bunk, 34, *34,* 36, 53, 54, *54,* 55
Johnson, William Geary. *See* Johnson, Bunk.
Jolson, Al, 16
Joplin, Scott, 18, 19, 20–21, *20*
Joseph, Charles Lee, 57
Joseph, Kirk Matthew, 57
Joseph, Waldron "Frog," 57

Keppard, Freddie, 36, 38, 44, 53
Krupa, Gene, 48

Ladnier, Tommy, 23, 34, 45, 47, 54
Laine, George Vitelle. *See* Laine, "Papa" Jack.
Laine, "Papa" Jack, 16, 19, 32, *32,* 33, 54
Lane, William Henry, 15
Lannigan, Jim, *48,* 49
LaRocca, Nick, 35, 40, *41,* 42, 54
Ledbetter, Huddy, 25, *25*
Lemott, Ferdinand. *See* Morton, Jelly Roll.
Lewis, Meade Lux, 58
Lomax, Alan, 9

Mahara's Minstrels, 16, 17
"Mamie's Blues," 9, 22
"Maple Leaf Rag," 18, 19, 20, 21
Marable, Fate, 35
Mares, Paul, 42
Mathews, Artie, 18
McCabe's Minstrels, 16, 34
McKinney, Bill, 50, *51*
McKinney's Cotton Pickers, 50–51
McPartland, Dick, *48,* 49

McPartland, Jimmy, *48,* 49
Mesirow, Milton. *See* Mezzrow, Mezz.
Mezzrow, Mezz, 47, *47,* 50, 54, 55
"Milenberg Joys," 9, 42, 50
Mingus, Charles, 59
Monk, Thelonious, 59
Morton, Jelly Roll, 6, 7, 8–9, 13, 16, 19, 22, 34, 35, 42, 44, 45, 54

New Orleans, 27–30
New Orleans jazz, 7, 37, 38, 40, 42, 43, 45, 46
festival, 57
New Orleans Rhythm Kings, 9, 42, 46, 49
Nicholas, Albert, 45
North, Dave, *48,* 49

O'Brien, Floyd, 48
Oliver, Harriet, 31
Oliver, Joe "King," 36–37, *36,* 38, 43–44, *43,* 45, *45,* 46, 53
Olympia Band, 33, 36
Original Creole Jazz Band, 37, 38, 44, 45
Original Dixieland Jazz Band, 17, 35, 41, 42, 52, 54
Ory, Edward "Kid," *36,* 37, 38, 54

Paul Whiteman Orchestra, 52, 58
Parker, Charlie "Yardbird," 59, *59*
Probert, George Arthur, 56

Ragas, Henry, *41*
Ragtime, 18–20
Rainey, Gertrude "Ma," *15,* 16, 22, *22,* 23, *23,* 24, 26
Rainey's Rabbit Foot Minstrels, *15,* 16, 23, 26
Ramsey, Frederick, 54, 55

Red Hot Peppers, 9, 45
Redman, Don, 50, 51
Reliance Brass Band, 32, *32,* 33
Robichaux, John, 19, 33
Russell, Pee Wee, 54, 55
Russell, William, 54, 55

Shields, Larry, 40, *41*
Sissle, Noble, 21
Slavery, 10–12, 27
Smith, Bessie, 16, 17, 23, 24, 26–27, *26*
Smith, Clara, 24
Smith, Mamie, 23
Smith, Pine Top (Clarence), 58
Sousa, John Philip, 18
Spanier, Francis Joseph. *See* Spanier, "Muggsy."
Spanier, "Muggsy," 46, *46*
Spargo, Tony, 40, *41*
Spivey, Victoria, 24, *24*
Stein's Dixie Jass Band, 40
"St. Louis Blues," 16, 17, 26
Storyville, 8, 30, 37
Stravinsky, Igor, 19–20
Superior Brass Band, *34*

Teagarden, Jack, 39, *44,* 48, 55
Teschemacher, Frank, *48,* 49
Tough, Dave, *48,* 49
Treemonisha, 20, 21
Trumbauer, Frank, 52, *52*
Turpin, Tom, 18

Wallace, Sippie, 24
Waller, Fats, 51
Whiteman, Paul, 58